Pebble® Plus

Habitats around the World

Life in the Desert

by Alison Auch

D1293884

CAPSTONE PRESS
a capstone imprint

Pebble Plus is published by Capstone Press,
1710 Roe Crest Drive, North Mankato, Minnesota 56003.
www.capstonepub.com

Library of Congress Cataloging-in-Publication Data
Auch, Alison.
  Life in the desert / by Alison Auch.
      p. cm. — (Pebble plus: Habitats around the world)
  Includes bibliographical references and index.
  Summary: "Color photos and simple text describe animals and their adaptations to a desert habitat"—Provided by
publisher.
  ISBN 978-1-4296-6817-0 (library binding)
  ISBN 978-1-4296-7150-7 (paperback)
  1. Desert ecology—Juvenile literature. 2. Desert animals—Juvenile literature. I. Title.
  QH541.5.D4A83 2012
  577.54—dc22   2011005316

Editorial Credits
Gillia Olson, editor; Lori Bye, designer; Svetlana Zhurkin, media researcher; Laura Manthe, production specialist

Photo Credits
Dreamstime/Majedali, 14–15; Michael Elliott, 20; Ron Chapple Studios, 5
Getty Images/National Geographic/Bruce Dale, 17
Photolibrary/Peter Arnold/Christophe Véchot, 10–11; Peter Arnold/Xavier Eichaker, 6–7
Shutterstock/EcoPrint, cover; Eldad Yitzhak, 9; Martha Marks, 1; Volodymyr Goinyk, 21
Visuals Unlimited/Joe McDonald, 13; Marli Miller, 18–19

Note to Parents and Teachers

The Habitats around the World series supports national science standards related to life science.
This book describes and illustrates animals that live in deserts. The images support early readers
in understanding the text. The repetition of words and phrases helps early readers learn new
words. This book also introduces early readers to subject-specific vocabulary words, which are
defined in the Glossary section. Early readers may need assistance to read some words and to
use the Table of Contents, Glossary, Read More, Internet Sites, and Index sections of the book.

Printed in the United States of America in North Mankato, Minnesota.
042017   010440R

Table of Contents

In the Desert

Deserts are thirsty places.

They get less than 10 inches

(25 centimeters) of rain a year.

Still, these dry places are

full of amazing animals.

Cool Body Parts

Some animals have body parts that help them beat the heat. Sand cats have thick fur on their feet. It keeps hot sand from burning their toes.

Lizards, snakes, and other reptiles do great in the desert. They have scaly, watertight skin. They don't sweat, so they don't lose water.

Finding Food

In hot deserts most animals hunt at night when it's cooler. Scorpions hunt insects and spiders. They use their tail stingers to kill prey.

Many desert animals get all their water from their food. Kangaroo rats get water from seeds. Falcons get water from the animals they eat.

Some desert animals are good at storing food for later. Gila monsters store fat in their tails to live off between meals. Camels store fat in their humps.

Homes

Some animals dig to escape
dry, hot weather. Fennec foxes
rest in burrows during the day.
Some toads stay buried
for months until it rains.

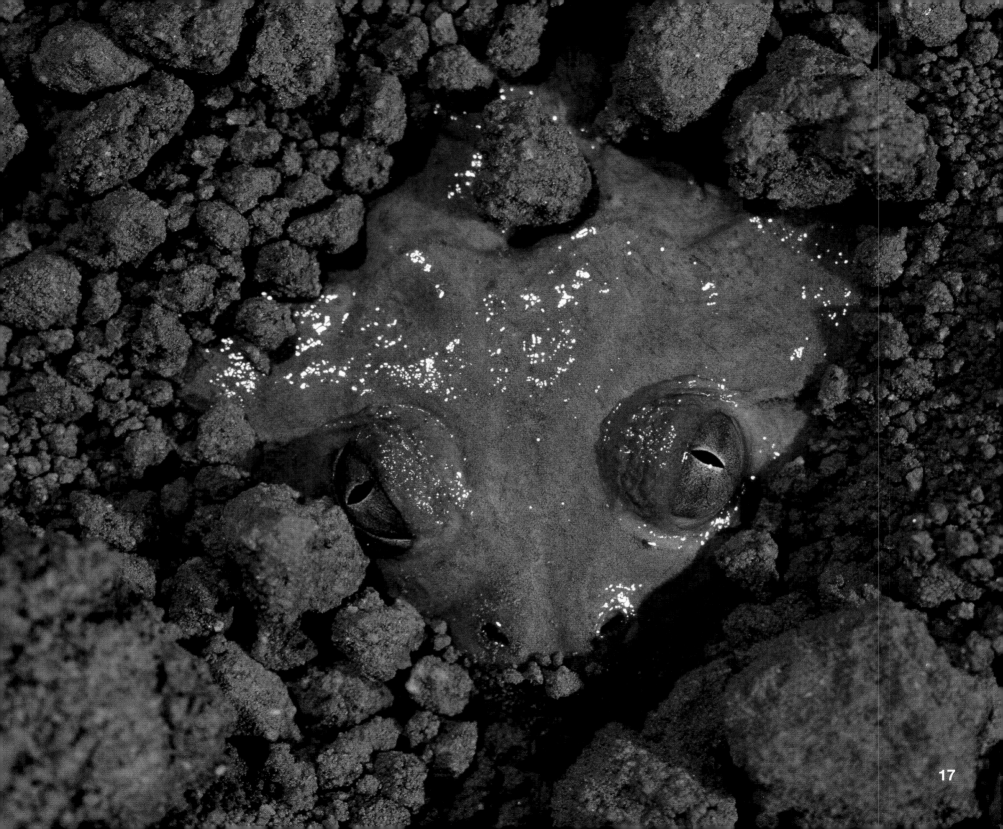

Pupfish live in desert springs. These tough fish can live in water that is nearly boiling! Amazing desert animals survive in even the toughest places.

pupfish

Fun Facts

* Fennec foxes have big ears for a reason. The extra skin allows heat to leave the body more easily.

* The Atacama Desert in Chile is the driest place on Earth. In one 20-year period, it rained only once.

* Camels are often called "ships of the desert." Riding a camel can feel like rolling on ocean waves.

✸ Not all deserts are hot.
Antarctica is the coldest place
on Earth, but it's very dry.
All the water stays frozen.

✸ During a desert's coldest months,
pupfish burrow into the bottom
of their springs. They come out
when it gets warmer.

Glossary

boiling—heated until bubbling; water boils when it reaches 212 degrees Fahrenheit (100 degrees Celsius)

burrow—a tunnel or hole in the ground where animals live; to burrow also means to dig in the ground

insect—a small animal with a hard outer shell, six legs, three body sections, and two antennae; most insects have wings

prey—an animal hunted by another animal for food

reptile—a cold-blooded animal that breathes air and has a backbone; most reptiles lay eggs and have scaly skin

spring—a place where water rises from underground and becomes a stream

stinger—a sharp, pointy part of an animal that can be used to sting

Read More

Ganeri, Anita. *Scorpion.* A Day in the Life: Desert Animals. Chicago: Heinemann Library, 2011.

Gray, Leon. *Deserts.* Geography Wise. New York: PowerKids Press, 2011.

Rustad, Martha E. H. *Animal Camouflage in the Desert.* Hidden in Nature. Mankato, Minn.: Capstone Press, 2010.

Vogel, Julia. *Desert Food Chains.* Fascinating Food Chains. Edina, Minn.: Magic Wagon, 2011.

Internet Sites

FactHound offers a safe, fun way to find Internet sites related to this book. All of the sites on FactHound have been researched by our staff.

Here's all you do:

Visit *www.facthound.com*

Type in this code: 9781429668170

Super-cool stuff!

Check out projects, games and lots more at
www.capstonekids.com

Index

Word Count: 201 (main text)

Grade: 1

Early-Intervention Level: 18